SNAKES
AS A NEW PET

JAKE OBERON

CONTENTS

P9-AOX-653

Photos by William B. Allen, Mr. C. Banks, W.R. Branch, Dr. Warren Burgess, M.J. Cox, Dr. Guido Dingerkus, John Dommers, Ron Everhart, Isabelle Francais, Michael Gilroy, R.T. Hoser, Burkhard Kahl, John T. Kellnhauser, S. Kochetov, courtesy R.E. Kunts, J.K. Langhammer, Gerard Marcuse, Ronald G. Markel, Dr. Sherman A. Minton, Aaron Norman, Suthigit Patramangor, Louis Porras, Robert T. Zappalorti.

Cover photos:
Front — The venomous adder, *Vipera berus.*
Back — The ornate flying snake, *Chrysopelea ornata.*
Inside Front — Eurasian grass snake, *Natrix natrix.*
Inside Back —Viperine water snake, *Natrix maura.*
Cover photos by Burkhard Kahl.

© Copyright 1990 by T.F.H. Publications, Inc.

Distributed in the UNITED STATES by T.F.H. Publications, Inc., One T.F.H. Plaza, Neptune City, NJ 07753; in CANADA to the Pet Trade by H & L Pet Supplies Inc., 27 Kingston Crescent, Kitchener, Ontario N2B 2T6; Rolf C. Hagen Ltd., 3225 Sartelon Street, Montreal 382 Quebec; in CANADA to the Book Trade by Macmillan of Canada (A Division of Canada Publishing Corporation), 164 Commander Boulevard, Agincourt, Ontario M1S 3C7; in ENGLAND by T.F.H. Publications, The Spinney, Parklands, Portsmouth PO7 6AR; in AUSTRALIA AND THE SOUTH PACIFIC by T.F.H. (Australia) Pty. Ltd., Box 149, Brookvale 2100 N.S.W., Australia; in NEW ZEALAND by Ross Haines & Son, Ltd., 82 D Elizabeth Knox Place, Panmure, Auckland, New Zealand; in the PHILIPPINES by Bio-Research, 5 Lippay Street, San Lorenzo Village, Makati, Rizal; in SOUTH AFRICA by Multipet Pty. Ltd., P.O. Box 35347, Northway, 4065, South Africa. Published by T.F.H. Publications, Inc. Manufactured in the United States of America by T.F.H. Publications, Inc.

Introduction

A member of the racer genus, *Coluber gemonensis*. These snakes are sometimes called whip snakes.

Snakes are probably the most maligned members of the Animal Kingdom, and many people shudder at the mere mention of the word. Ironically, most of those people who profess a fear or dislike of snakes know next to nothing about them and probably do not want to know. Indeed, they usually have very little interest in natural history whatsoever. They would not know, for example, that all animals and plants play an important part in the ecology of a given area — and snakes are no exception.

The universal fear and loathing of serpents is understandable and probably stems from our ancestors, who lived much closer to nature than most of us do now. Even today, in some countries where poor people often walk unshod, death or serious injury from the bite of a venomous snake is not an unusual occurrence. However, of the 2800 or so species of snakes known to man, only about 10% are venomous and an even smaller proportion is fatally dangerous.

There are a large number of bizarre and sometimes ridiculous snake stories in circulation, again usually put about by people who know nothing about reptiles and their habits. Most of these stories originated in the distant past and, amazingly, in spite of our ever increasing general knowledge of the creatures with which we share our planet, they still persist. Here are just three of the "old wives' tales" that can be discounted at a stroke:

False: If you kill a king cobra you will be relentlessly pursued by its mate until revenge is meted.

False: The coachwhip snake will bind an adversary to a tree trunk with its coils, then proceed mercilessly to whip him to death with its tail.

False: The "bootlace snake" disguises itself on your boots or shoes at night, ready to bite you between the fingers when you put your shoes on; death follows in seconds.

These quotes and many similar ones are of course nonsensical, but anyone who is interested enough to study snakes in their own right will find that their true life histories are almost as fantastic as the superstitions that abound. In recent years a growing number of snake fanciers have put aside their prejudices and taken a more positive attitude toward these much-maligned creatures. A greater awareness of wildlife and its conservation, much publicized by the media, has recently changed the attitudes of many people. Even those creatures that were formerly discounted as mere "creepy crawlies" are now being viewed with a greater benevolence.

Corn snake, *Elaphe guttata*. This species is a favorite, as it is relatively easy to keep in captivity.

Mexican kingsnake hatchlings, *Lampropeltis mexicanus*. Note the difference in the coloration and scale pattern between these two siblings.

City dwellers, whose opportunities of visiting the countryside are few and far between, have taken to keeping a little bit of nature in their apartments. There are those who keep an array of exotic house plants; others have tropical aquaria containing a lush display of aquatic vegetation and jewel-like fishes; and there is a comparatively new band of enthusiasts who prefer to keep a terrarium containing a living display of plants and reptiles or other terrestrial creatures.

There is no doubt that snakes are steadily gaining in popularity as household pets. There is such a great variety of sizes, colors, patterns, habits, and temperaments that there is something to suit everybody. There are those that are very easy to keep, feed, breed, and require no more than a few minutes of maintenance each day; conversely, there are those that are more difficult to care for, perhaps due to their specialized habitats or diets, but constitute a challenge to the keen herpetologist.

Snakes have much to recommend them over the more conventional pets such as dogs, cats, or birds. They do not require a great deal of space; indeed, there are different sizes of snake for different spaces. One can build or purchase a terrarium of a size designed to fit into a particular alcove, then decide which snake species are suitable for those accommodations. Snakes do not smell, providing they are kept in clean conditions; they do not make excessive noise; nor do they require to be taken out for walks. Maintenance in a carefully designed exhibit should take no more than a few minutes each day. Once the basic terrarium has been set up satisfactorily, it should not be excessively expensive. An attractively set up, well maintained terrarium, complete with exotic plants and a pair of colorful serpents, can be very decorative and will complement the decor of any living space. Not least, terraria provide an endless conversational topic when visitors arrive.

In this little book the author will try to dispel the various prejudices that the prospective snake keeper or his family may have against acquiring a pet snake, offering an introduction to their biology and a concise guide to their captive care and feeding. The subject of breeding snakes is beyond the scope of this book, but the topic is important to experienced snake-keepers. Every specimen bred in captivity and passed on to another snake keeper will mean one fewer collected from the wild. The ideal situation will be when there are enough captive-bred specimens to supply demand, thus precluding altogether the necessity of wild collections, which can only further increase the already serious vulnerability of many species.

One of the mangrove snakes, *Boiga jaspidea.* Some members of the genus *Boiga* have potent venom and are not recommended for hobbyists.

Snake Herpetology

The boa constrictor, *Boa constrictor*, has been kept in captivity for many generations.

The word "herpetology" was coined from the ancient Greek *herpeton,* which was applied to any creature of a lowly, creeping status. Today herpetology describes the study of amphibians and reptiles. Anyone who has an interest in snakes should also have an interest in basic herpetology at least as it will lead to a more general understanding of the serpent's origins and habits. In this book we will confine our study of herpetology to the basics, but with particular application to the snakes.

SNAKE EVOLUTION

Snakes are reptiles, sharing the zoological class Reptilia with the Chelonia (turtles, terrapins, and tortoises), the Crocodylia (crocodiles, alligators, and gavial), the Rhynchocephalia (tuatara), and the Lacertilia (lizards). All reptiles originally arose from the Amphibia, which themselves evolved from certain fish-like ancestors some 370 million years ago during the late Devonian period. Although the pioneers of terrestrial vertebrate life, the amphibians have never totally lost their dependence on water both for normal day-to-day existence and, particularly, for reproduction. The amphibian skin is semi-permeable, which means that its owner is unable to live in arid conditions without perishing from loss of body fluids through evaporation. Most amphibians require fresh water in which to reproduce. As a general rule (with many exceptions), fertilization is external and the male spermatozoa must be transferred to the female ova in a watery environment. Also dependent on water is the subsequent development of the egg and the larva to the adult form. Without free water this metamorphosis could not take place.

Some 70 million years after the appearance of the first amphibians, most of which were large, squat, somewhat salamander-like creatures, the first reptiles appeared. One of the earliest genera is known as *Limnoscelis,* and its fossil remains have many characteristics in common with some of the labyrinthodont amphibians from which it is assumed it evolved. These events took place toward the end of the Carboniferous (Pennsylvanian) period. During the Permian, which immediately followed, colonization of the dry land by numerous new and progressively more advanced species of reptile was in its hey-day. By studying the fossilized evidence from this period, paleontologists have

Dog-toothed mangrove snake, *Boiga cynodon.* This species feeds mainly on birds; therefore, satisfying its dietary needs may not be easy.

been able to draw up a fairly accurate picture of early reptilian evolution.

The reptiles were the first vertebrates to permanently colonize the dry land. They developed certain adaptations that enabled them to complete their life cycles without dependence on large bodies of water. These adaptations include a

Asiatic rock python, *Python molurus bivittatus*, with eggs. All pythons are egg-layers rather than live-bearers.

dry, scaly skin that is barely permeable and minimizes fluid loss through evaporation; the ability to excrete nitrogenous waste in the form of insoluble uric acid, thus saving more water; the advent of internal fertilization, in which the

male spermatozoa are transferred directly into the female cloaca; and, most importantly, the development of the *cleidoic* egg (an egg enclosed within a protective shell, containing its own watery environment, a supply of nutrients, and other adaptations to ensure the welfare of the developing embryo). With these adaptations, reptiles were able to colonize areas of the earth's surface that amphibians are unable to tolerate.

All of the reptilian orders that occur today arose during the Triassic period, which immediately followed the Permian; other orders that arose at the time are now long extinct. The order Squamata, which includes all of the modern lizards and snakes, arose at this time and soon gained the distinction of being the most successful of reptile groups, at least with regard to the abundance of the species and individuals, the range of adaptations, and the geographical distribution. The snakes were the last of all reptiles to evolve, but, unfortunately, the fossil history of serpents is very fragmentary due to the fragility of the bones that are often scattered over a wide area. Vertebrae are often common when searched for, however, and many fossil species have been described from isolated vertebrae. Much of our knowledge of snake evolution is inferred from the study of the comparative anatomy of

(about 125 million years ago). Another significant find was the complete fossil snake *Dinilysia patagonica,* from the Upper Cretaceous sandstone beds of Argentina. This bears a number of similarities to the modern *Cylindrophis* and also has a number of primitive lizard-like characteristics.

Bull snake, *Pituophis melanoleucus.* Members of this genus require a warm, dry terrarium habitat.

modern forms, but it can be safely assumed that snakes evolved from lacertilian (lizard-like) ancestors.

The earliest recognizable snake remains are a number of vertebrae classified as *Lapparentophis defrennei* found in the Sahara and reputed to be from the Lower Cretaceous period

SNAKE CLASSIFICATION

With the infinite variety of life on this planet, it is obvious that to avoid confusion scientists require a system of classifying the myriad species. Several attempts have been made at classifying the animal and plant kingdoms, but it was

9

Corn snake, *Elaphe guttata*. This creature is amelanistic or albino, which means the normal black pigment has been reduced, creating a snake of a different color.

the Swedish botanist Carl Linnaeus who, toward the end of the eighteenth century, pioneered the system in use today. Every species was given a two part name, based on classical Latin or Greek. The first part of the name comprises the *genus* and the second part the *trivial* or *species name.* Based on differences and similarities, species are grouped together into genera, genera into families, families into orders, orders into classes, and so on. Taking snakes as an example, the following table shows how the corn snake, *Elaphe guttata,* is classified in the animal kingdom:

Kingdom – Animalia – All animals

Phylum – Chordata – All chordates

Subphylum – Vertebrata – All backboned animals

Superclass – Tetrapoda – Four-limbed animals

Class – Reptilia – All reptiles

Order – Squamata – All snakes and lizards

Suborder – Serpentes – All snakes

Family – Colubridae – Typical snakes

Genus – *Elaphe* – Rat snakes

Species – *Elaphe guttata* – Corn snake

Subspecies – *Elaphe guttata emoryi* – Great Plains ratsnake

It will be seen in the table that a further rank, the subspecies, is placed below the species. Subspecific rank designates populations (usually separate portions of a species range) that show certain characteristic differences that are great enough to classify but are not sufficiently prominent to warrant separate specific rank. Another peculiarity of the table is that snakes are classed as Tetrapoda (four-limbed animals) in spite of the fact that they are limbless. This is because snakes are reptiles, all of which were four-limbed at

some stage of their ancestry.

People who study the classification of living organisms are known as *taxonomists* and, as in any scientific discipline, there is frequently a certain amount of argument as to how a particular species should be classified. That is why different books about snakes may show apparent differences in their methods of classification. In this book, the snakes will be classified into families, as listed in the table below.

ANATOMY AND BIOLOGY OF SNAKES

The most significant feature of snakes is their lack of limbs. There is no pectoral girdle in any

Common or black racer, *Coluber constrictor*. Racers require adequate hiding places in their captive environment.

Yellow rat snake, *Elaphe obsoleta quadrivittata*. Some rat snakes will remain aggressive throughout their lives.

11

Family	Approximate Number of Genera	Approximate Number of Species
1 Typhlopidae (Blind snakes)	5	200
2 Leptotyphlopidae (Thread snakes)	2	50
3 Aniliidae (Cylinder snakes)	3	10
4 Uropeltidae (Shield tails)	8	40
5 Boidae (Boas and pythons)	22	90
6 Xenopeltidae (Sunbeam snake)	1	1
7 Acrochordidae (Wart snakes)	1	3
8 Colubridae (Typical snakes)	250	2300
9 Elapidae (Cobras, coral snakes and mambas)	41	180
10 Hydrophiidae (Sea snakes)	16	50
11 Viperidae (Vipers and pit vipers)	14	150

Rat snakes vary from species to species. Some are ground-dwellers while others live in trees; some feed on frogs or fish while others prefer small mammals and birds.

species, but some of the primitive families have vestigial remnants of a pelvis and may have traces of a femur. In the Boidae, the vestigial femur manifests itself as a claw-like appendage on either side of the vent. These "claws" or spurs seem to play some significance in the mating behavior of pythons, the male using them to stimulate the female by scratching her skin. Apart from this pelvic

A trio of green tree pythons, *Chondropython viridis*, an adult with young. Juveniles are yellow, orange, red, or brown; they turn green with age.

girdle in some of the primitive families, the skeleton of a snake consists solely of a skull and a vertebral column extending right along the body to the tip of the tail. With the exception of some of the first vertebrae in the neck and those of the tail, each vertebrae is furnished with a pair of jointed, mobile ribs that form the cylindrical body cavity.

The whole of the snake's body is covered with a series of hard, often glossy, scales that are really specialized thickened folds of the skin. The scales are overlapping, with the "open" end toward the rear, thus allowing for efficient forward movement in the rocks and undergrowth. With the exception of the sea snakes and a few aquatic (water-dwelling) and burrowing species, most serpents possess wide belly scales (ventrals) that span the width of the underside. These scales are important in the snake's unique method of locomotion. The vertebrae, with their accessory articulating facets and the long ribs, are attached to these broad belly scales by a complex muscle system. By expanding and contracting these muscles in a peristaltic (wave-like) motion along the body, the belly scales catch on irregularities in the substrate and propel the reptile forward. Increase in speed is accomplished by lateral undulations of the body that press against solid

13

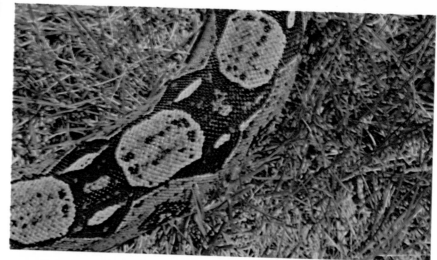

Top: Dorsal view of the scales of a boa constrictor, *Boa constrictor.* *Bottom:* Ventral view of the same snake.

objects. This explains why a snake has difficulty in moving quickly over a smooth, obstacle-free area but is able to disappear with remarkable rapidity when spotted in undergrowth or rocky areas. In spite of this apparent speed, snakes are incapable of outpacing a man or a four-footed animal in an obstacle-free area.

Certain desert-dwelling species, for example the sidewinder, *Crotalus cerastes,* have developed a method of locomotion known as sidewinding; this is accomplished by throwing loops of the body forward, enabling the reptile to move with some efficiency over loose, sandy soil.

The hard, horn-like consistency of the scales hinders the sustained growth of snakes, so the outer epidermis has to be replaced at frequent intervals, usually some three to six times per year. The regular shedding or sloughing of the skin in snakes is known as ecdysis or molting. As the snake grows (which it does all of its life, though the rate decreases with age) its skin becomes dull and the pattern often becomes less distinct. A couple of days before shedding, a lubricating fluid is secreted between the old outer epidermis and the new skin beneath. This is especially noticeable under the brill (the transparent eye spectacle, which is really a specialized scale covering and protecting the lidless eye), where a milky cloudiness will be seen. When the reptile is ready to shed, it loosens the skin around the lips by rubbing them against a rough surface such as a rock or the bark of a tree. When the skin of the head is sufficiently loose, the serpent will crawl out of the old skin by jamming its body into some convenient crevice. The old skin is turned inside out in the process and, in a healthy shed, should remain intact. Certain problems derived from inefficient shedding will be dealt with later in the text. The newly shed snake is a sleek, colorful edition of its dull former self.

A unique characteristic of

The house snake, *Boaedon fuliginosus*, is an egg-layer that feeds on frogs, lizards, mammals, and birds.

Viperine snake, *Natrix maura*. The shape of a snake's jaws tells much about the type of diet it requires and about its lifestyle in general.

the snake's skull is the elastic joints of the various bones that enable the reptile to swallow whole prey sometimes considerably larger than the head itself. The elastic joints of the upper and lower jaws are set relatively far back, allowing a huge gape. The two halves of the lower jaw are loosely connected at the chin with elastic tissue, allowing independent movement of each mandible. The brain is totally enclosed by bone, but the palate bones are movable, thus decreasing the risk of brain damage when large prey is being swallowed.

All snakes are carnivorous and do not willingly take vegetable food. As they take whole prey animals, this constitutes a balanced diet within itself. Snakes have various methods of hunting, catching, and overpowering prey, depending on the species, but all have varying numbers of sharp, backwardly curving teeth, making it difficult for struggling prey to escape once they have been seized. The most important aspect of prey detection in snakes is the sense of smell, although

A juvenile racer, *Coluber constrictor*. Most racers grow darker with age.

sight may play a part in some species. All snakes have a highly mobile forked tongue with which they are continually testing the environment by flicking it out through a small opening (labial aperture) at the front of the closed mouth. Scent particles are picked up from the air or from solid objects and conveyed to the palate by the tips of the tongue. In the palate there are two sacs, the Jacobson's organs; the tips of the tongue apply the scent particles to these sacs, which are connected to the olfactory nerves and convey a message to the brain, informing the snake of the presence of prey, of danger, of water, or of a mate.

Having detected prey, the simplest method of

overpowering it in many snake species is to grab and swallow; this method is commonly used by smaller snakes that feed on invertebrates or small vertebrates. Larger snakes, such as the boids and some colubrids that have to deal with more powerful, potentially dangerous prey, practice constriction. This is accomplished by first grabbing the prey in the mouth and then throwing coils of the body around it. As the prey struggles the coils are progressively tightened until the prey dies of asphyxiation, after which it is swallowed.

The most advanced forms of snakes, including the rear-fanged colubrids, the elapids, the hydrophiids, and the viperids, possess venom fangs with which to subdue and kill their prey. Snakes are sometimes categorized by the arrangement of their teeth and fangs. All non-venomous species that are solid toothed are classed as *aglyphus;* the rear-fanged colubrids (formerly a subfamily, Boiginae) that have grooved venom fangs toward the rear of the jaw are classed as *opisthoglyphus*; the Elapidae and the Hydrophiidae, which have a pair of rigid fangs with partially closed venom canals set at the front of the upper jaw, are classed as *proteroglyphus;* and the snakes with the most advanced form of teeth, the Viperidae, have hinged fangs with fully closed venom canals at the front of the jaw and are termed *solenoglyphus.* There are many exceptions to these categories, and they are no longer used formally by taxonomists. Venomous snakes may hang on to weaker prey after striking and allow the venom to take effect while holding it in the mouth. Most rear-fangs have to actively "chew" on their prey to introduce venom. More robust prey is usually released after striking. The snake will wait for a few minutes for the venom to take effect before tracking it down by scent. In all venomous snakes the paired venom glands are situated in the cheeks just behind the eyes and the venom is forced along the grooves or through the canals in the fangs by the contraction of the gland

Corn snake, *Elaphe guttata.*

casing.

The eyesight of snakes varies greatly, depending on the species; some of the burrowing snakes are virtually blind, with mere vestiges of eyes. Most of the more advanced snakes have reasonable eyesight that is oriented to detect movement. A few species (*Ahaetulla nasuta,* the long-nosed tree snake, for example) have binocular vision that enables them to recognize even non-moving prey by sight.

Snakes do not have external ears or eardrums and therefore are incapable of hearing in the sense that we know it. They do not pick up airborne sounds, but due to their closeness with the substrate they are able to "hear" vibrations caused by the movement of other animals or by the action of wind and water.

Some snakes, including many of the boids and the pit vipers (Crotalidae) have an additional sense for detecting prey. These are the infrared heat-detecting pits, the labial pits, that are present around the lips of some boids and between the eye and the nostril of pit vipers. These concavities, either in or between the scales, are lined with much thinner skin and are richly supplied with nerve endings. Experiments have shown that such snakes, even with their senses of sight and scent out of action, are capable of detecting accurately the location of warm-blooded prey and can react to temperature differences of less than 1°C.

Snakes possess most of the essential internal organs that other vertebrates possess, but these must, of course, be modified to fit into the elongated, cylindrical body. There usually is only one functional lung, the right

Eurasian water snake, *Natrix natrix helvetica.* Members of this genus have large eyes and large teeth.

Common garter snake, *Thamnophis sirtalis tetrataenia.*

one, that is elongated and passes for a considerable distance along the trunk. The left lung is vestigial or absent except in very primitive families. The liver is likewise elongated and does not possess lobes. There is a gall bladder. The kidneys of the snake are band-like and placed almost behind each other. There is no bladder; urine is passed directly into the cloaca, where it is voided in nearly solid form through the vent together with the feces.

All reptiles, including snakes, are sometimes described as being "cold-blooded." This term can be somewhat misleading, as a reptile's blood can be quite warm; it all depends on the environmental temperature. Unlike the mammals and the birds, which are endotherms and regulate their body temperature from within and, under normal circumstances, keep them fairly constant, the reptiles (and the fishes and the amphibians) are ectotherms and must rely on external heat sources to gain body heat. Snakes do have a

performance of its biological functions.

With the exception of the polar regions and very high altitudes where permafrost precludes the possibility of frost-free hibernation below the surface, snakes have colonized most suitable areas of the earth's surface. There are burrowing snakes, water snakes, sea snakes, desert snakes, and tree snakes, each of which has evolved special adaptations for its own particular life style. Many of these adaptations have to be borne in mind when considering the housing and management of captive specimens.

Above: Rainbow boa, *Epicrates cenchria*. The iridescent quality of this snake's scales must be seen to be believed. *Right:* Mangrove snake, *Boiga kraepelini*.

preferred average body temperature that they are able to maintain by moving in and out (as by basking) of the sun's rays or other warm places such as under flat stones or in rotting logs. The preferred body temperature varies from species to species, depending on the climate and habitat in which it lives, but it is important for the reptile to maintain the optimum temperature required for the efficient

Housing

Example of a simple terrarium set-up which includes newspaper substrate, water dish, and cardboard box hiding place. Such a cage is ideal as a quarantine station for newly acquired snakes.

Typical housing for captive snakes is a container that is usually referred to as either a terrarium or a vivarium. The general requirements of a terrarium are that it should be escape-proof and of sufficient size to allow the species being kept to move about and behave as naturally as possible. There should be means of maintaining suitable temperatures, adequate lighting, a correct level of humidity, and sufficient draft-free ventilation combined to form a micro-climate suitable for the species being kept. In addition, the terrarium should be so constructed that

23

Pine snake, *Pituophis melanoleucus*, in a terrarium with water dish, branch for climbing, and plastic jar for hiding.

habitat and habits of the species to be kept should be studied by referring to field guides, to climatic graphs in an atlas, and to papers in herpetological journals, or by communicating directly with those who have already experienced success with the species in question. Should one wish to keep species of varying climatic requirements, then it will be necessary to have several terraria, each of a design suitable for one individual type. There are no standard requirements that can be laid down when one considers the huge range of habitats, climates, and foods of the different snake species.

Terraria may be constructed from a wide range of materials, but basically they are enclosed, escape-proof areas with at least one side of glass so that the interior may be observed. One of the simplest forms of terrarium is a simple fish tank (without water, of course) with a secure lid or hood into which heat and light sources can be installed. As ventilation of such tanks cannot come from the sides, it is important that a large

it is easy to maintain (with regard to feeding, cleaning, and control of the inmates) and should be attractive enough to enhance or be the focal point in the room in which it is kept.

TERRARIA

It is possible to purchase ready-made terraria complete with all the necessary equipment from pet shops and specialist suppliers, but it is often much more practical, as well as being more fun, to design and construct a cage to one's own specifications. The terrarium can be made a specific shape or size to fit into the available space, and the various life-support systems can be designed to suit specific species. Before creating a terrarium, the area of the lid be ventilated. This can be accomplished by drilling numerous small holes or by cutting out a large hole and covering it with strong plastic or metal mesh. For small snakes, a simple plastic aquarium is useful. Such tanks are cheap and are particularly suitable for rearing large numbers of juvenile specimens. The tanks may be arranged on racks in a heated room. The major disadvantages of using aquaria as terraria are that they lose heat very fast (glass is a fine conductor of heat) and are difficult to adjust to the proper humidity.

Another popular type of terrarium, more suitable to those species requiring arid conditions, is constructed from plywood. It is basically a box with a wooden framed glass door in the front. There are a number of variations on this theme. The terrarium can be made to any size and can be tall for tree snakes or low for terrestrial species. If you obtain a large plastic cat-litter tray you can construct the terrarium to fit

Flower snake, *Elaphe moellendorffi*, member of the rat snake genus. This species originates in southern China and prefers well-heated quarters.

around this so that you have a waterproof floor that can slide out for cleaning. The viewing glass can either be set into a hinged, solid frame or the glass itself can simply slide into grooved frames at the sides or the top and bottom. The latter method is better when you intend to have terraria stacked above each other. The best method of constructing a plywood terrarium is to use half-inch marine or exterior plywood that is tacked and glued together. The interior surface should be primed and receive an undercoat, then apply a topcoat of good quality lead-free gloss paint that should be allowed at least one week to dry out in a ventilated situation before any animals are introduced. The outside of the terrarium is most attractive if stained and varnished. Ventilation holes can be drilled in the sides and the roof or larger, fine-meshed ventilators may be fitted over large cut outs. It is probably safest to screen *all* ventilation holes even if they look so small that "no snake could possibly squeeze through there."

Lately many manufacturers have begun to market terraria — actually snake cages — made of fiberglass and Plexiglas. Although expensive, such cages have many advantages of design and materials over traditional cages and should last practically forever.

The lid of the terrarium should be made of wood or metal with ventilation panels and should have a facility

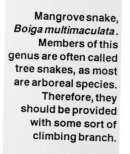

Mangrove snake, *Boiga multimaculata*. Members of this genus are often called tree snakes, as most are arboreal species. Therefore, they should be provided with some sort of climbing branch.

26

Royal python, *Python regius*. This species is a tree-dweller some of the time; therefore, it should have something to climb on.

for holding the heating/ lighting apparatus, which should preferably be concealed. The lid should fit tightly over the top of the terrarium and should have some means of securing it, commonly lugs cemented to the glass with sealer.

An aqua-terrarium is one in which semi-aquatic species are kept. These are preferably constructed wholly from glass or fiberglass, and a sheet of glass can be cemented across the width of the tank in the base to separate the land from the aquatic areas. For most semi-aquatic species the ratio should be approximately half land and half water. The land area can be prepared in much the same way as for a terrestrial tank. For reasons of hygiene, the aquatic section is best left devoid of any substrate materials; the water will have to be replaced frequently. For some small snakes, however, a power filter installed to clean the water will reduce the frequency with which it needs to be changed. It is usually a waste of time trying to grow aquatic plants in an aqua-terrarium as the snakes will soon uproot them.

DIMENSIONS OF TERRARIA

The dimensions given in the following table are guidelines only, and it is often a matter of trial and error before one arrives at a suitably sized terrarium for the various species. The sizes given are the minimum requirements for a pair of reptiles. The shape of the tank will depend on whether they are terrestrial, aquatic, or arboreal.

ENVIRONMENTAL SYSTEMS

The environmental systems in the terrarium that usually have to be supplied by artificial means include heating, lighting, humidity, and ventilation.

HEATING

As reptiles are poikilothermic (cold-blooded), they seek out their own preferred temperatures by moving in and out of sunlight or locations that are heated by the sun. In the indoor terrarium it is almost impossible to utilize natural sunlight for this purpose — if you allow sunlight to enter through the glass of the terrarium, there is a danger of overheating. Therefore, we have to provide heating by artificial means. Having found out about the wild habitat of the snakes in question, we will know what range of temperatures they are likely to require and we must give them this range artificially. By heating just one end of the terrarium we try to create a temperature gradient from the heated end to the unheated end. By experimenting with a thermometer and various

Artist's rendering of an arboreal set-up for tree-climbing snakes. This particular model is built into the wall.

heating appliances in the terrarium before the animals are introduced, it will be possible to arrive at a suitable range. There are many kinds of heating appliances that may be chosen on their merits or cheapness.

Tungsten Bulbs: Ordinary incandescent light bulbs with a tungsten element have long been the most frequently used means of heating (and lighting) the terrarium. As they emit yellow light they are recommended only as supplementary forms of lighting. However, their heating qualities in small spaces are very useful, and

Some species can be kept outdoors for part of the year if their terrarium is very secure—it must be escape-proof and amply defended against intrusion from other animals.

Length of snake		Minimum capacity		Sample dimensions	
1 ft.	30 cm	1 cu. ft	27 L	1x1x1 ft.	30x30x30 cm
2 ft.	60 cm	2 cu. ft	54 L	2x1x1 ft.	60x30x30 cm
3 ft.	90 cm	4 cu. ft	108 L	4x1x1 ft.	120x30x30 cm
5 ft.	150 cm	16 cu. ft	432 L	4x2x2 ft.	120x60x60 cm
10 ft.	300 cm	54 cu. ft	1460 L	5x3x3 ft.	180x90x90 cm

Plastic food containers can be modified for use as *temporary* quarters for newly hatched snakes.

they can be used alone or in conjunction with other appliances to maintain temperatures at suitable levels. The advantages of these bulbs are that they are cheap, readily available, and come in a range of sizes. The size of bulb used will depend on the amount of space to be heated and the temperature requirements of the inmates, but by experimenting with various wattages a suitable temperature range will be produced. Many snakes, particularly those from temperate and desert regions, benefit from a considerable drop in temperature at night. In most cases, this can be simply accomplished by switching off the bulb at the appropriate time and switching it on again the following morning. By using an automatic timer and a dimmer switch, a degree of imitation of dawn and dusk can be accomplished. The ambient temperature in the average home is adequate at night to support an unheated terrarium, but if there is a danger of excessively low temperatures at night a second bulb, blue or red in color and of lower wattage, can be switched on when the main light bulb is switched off. Due to the light factor, it is not suitable to have a tungsten bulb controlled by a thermostat; the light switching on and off during the daytime is likely to confuse the snakes. If a tungsten bulb is required for heating only, it can be concealed inside a container such as a clay plant pot, a metal can, or anything that will absorb the heat and re-radiate it. It is then safe to use a thermostat, which should be placed in part of the terrarium away from the heat source.

Infra-red Lamps: Infra-red lamps of the type used by breeders of pigs and other domestic animals are useful for large terraria. There are those that emit red light, others white light, but both emit radiant heat that is capable of heating surfaces to high temperatures. Such lamps are ideal for desert species that bask. The amount of heat is adjusted by raising or lowering the lamp over the basking area. The lamps are best situated outside the terrarium and directed through a metal gauze ventilator in the lid. This not only keeps the temperature of the basking area at a suitable level, but also it prevents the reptiles from touching the lamp and burning themselves. Before performing cleaning chores

in and around the terrarium, lamps should always be switched off and allowed to cool, otherwise droplets of water touching the lamps will cause them to burst.

Heating Pads and Cables: It is possible to purchase various heating pads and cables that are manufactured for aquarist or horticulturist use. The former may be placed under the terrarium and will heat the floor and the substrate. The latter are buried in the substrate itself. It is best to heat only half of the terrarium floor, thus

Emerald tree boa, *Corallus caninus*, in a typical pose. It is recommended that quarters for this species contain terrarium plants in addition to ample climbing branches.

confines of the tank will reduce the moisture a bit, this is insufficient for many desert reptiles kept in areas where the outside air is very humid (as in much of the United States most of the year). Some hobbyists have even tried using small desiccator units with limited success. Fortunately, few snakes are as sensitive to humidity as are many desert lizards. Maintaining a high humidity is much simpler most of the time. A glass cover on a glass terrarium will increase humidity markedly, especially if the

A wide variety of terraria, food and water dishes, and plants and other amenities are available at your local pet shop.

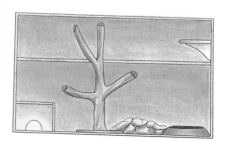

terrarium is misted once or twice a day. Pans of water allowed to evaporate also increase humidity. The high natural humidity of most terraria is the main reason most common houseplants do not survive in terraria.

VENTILATION

Good ventilation in the terrarium is essential to prevent a build up of stale air and to ensure that the inmates have a good oxygen supply. Provided we have adequate ventilation panels in the walls and lid, convection currents created by the heating apparatus will ensure satisfactory air replacement. Terraria should not be placed in a position where they will receive cold drafts. Also, terraria with totally screened tops tend to be much drier than those with glass tops, which will affect what types of snakes can be kept in any style of terrarium.

TERRARIUM DECORATION

There are two things to think about when furnishing a terrarium. There are the bare essentials that are necessary for the well-being of the animals, and there are the decorative items that may be added for esthetic purposes. The terrarium keeper with several tanks, perhaps based in a special breeding room, will want to keep furnishings as simple as possible in order to save time during routine cleaning chores. However, most enthusiasts will also want to have a decorative setup as a focal point in the living room or den. Remember, however, that elaborately decorated terraria are difficult to clean and lead to an "I'll do it tomorrow" attitude that can rapidly lead to dirty, smelly, disease-ridden cages. Most experienced herpetologists prefer a spartan cage with minimal accessories — a climbing branch, basking rock, water bowl, and hide box.

Substrate Materials: The simplest and most hygienic form of floor covering is absorbent paper. Disposable kitchen towels are ideal; these are simply placed on the floor of the cage and changed as soon as they become soiled. Newspaper is also satisfactory (and cheap), though somewhat

unattractive. More permanent and attractive floor coverings, although less hygienic, include various grades of gravel, processed corn cob materials, mixtures of coarse sand and peat, leaf litter, or bark chips. Gravel should be removed and washed at regular intervals, while the latter materials should be frequently changed. Except for paper and the new processed corn cob substrate materials, all other substrates are considered unsafe by at least some herpetologists — sand or gravel can be eaten by accident and block the intestines; leaf litter is loaded with bacteria and parasites; bark chips can be abrasive and are wonderful homes for mites.

Above: Corn snake, *Elaphe guttata*.

Below: One example of an uncluttered terrarium that contains all the necessities for many species.

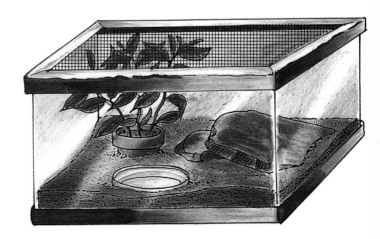

Climbing Branches: Stout climbing branches are essential for arboreal species. These should be fixed firmly into position so

Young variegated racer, *Coluber ravergieri.* Most racer species can be wintered outdoors if suitable supplemental heating is provided.

provide plastic or cardboard boxes with a hole cut in the side. The former may easily be cleaned, the latter disposed of and replaced

that they do not fall when the reptiles are climbing on them. Such branches should be scrubbed clean (and preferably boiled a bit) before use and then at regular intervals thereafter.

Basking Rocks: Almost all snakes (except for smaller burrowers and strictly nocturnal species) will use a flat rock or similar surface for basking, especially if it is placed under or near the light. Basking is a regular part of the behavior of many common snakes, including aquatic species, and should be provided to assure the health of the snake.

Hide Boxes: Many species of snakes like to spend their inactive times curled up in some cavity. The simplest method in the terrarium is to

when they become soiled. More natural hiding places include hollow logs and cavities in rocks. Both have disadvantages: logs harbor parasites and rocks collapse. When using rocks in the terrarium care should be taken to ensure that they cannot fall and injure the inmates. Silicone cement can be used to hold the rocks together. It is best that the box be a bit too small rather than much too large.

Water Containers: Containers of water are essential for most species (except dry desert types) for drinking or bathing purposes, or both. Many species of snakes like to spend long periods soaking in water, so a large shallow water container is essential.

For smaller species, earthenware or glass casserole dishes are ideal. For larger species a large plastic bowl may be used or, for a more natural effect a "pond" may be constructed from cement mortar and rocks. For very large boids, such a pond is almost essential and should preferably have a drain incorporated. While some snakes will drink from open containers, others survive on dew that condenses on their bodies or on plant leaves. You will have to check the literature to determine if your snake has to drink or be misted each day.

Plants: Plants in the terrarium can be very attractive and will enhance the appearance of the animals. However, it is almost impossible to keep plants in a terrarium with large snakes as their weight will destroy them. For small species, an attempt can be made to reproduce as nearly as possible the wild habitat. Tree snakes can be provided with robust plants on which to climb. Many "houseplants" will turn black and rot in the high humidity of terraria.

Bromeliads and other "air plants" will succeed in some humid terraria, while a desert terrarium could have one or two cacti or succulent plants tastefully placed among sand and rocks.

Plants are preferably left in their pots, which can be concealed behind rocks or logs. It is best to have spare plants so that they can be changed around, giving those that have been in the terrarium a chance to recuperate on the windowsill or in the greenhouse. Remember that plants require almost as much care as the animals and will want feeding and watering as well as the correct quota of light and temperature.

It is great fun to use one's

Corn snake, *Elaphe guttata*. Not only is water essential for drinking, but it is also necessary for many snakes to bathe in, especially during the shedding process.

artistic talents in designing and laying out a terrarium. Always ensure that the basic design is kept as simple as possible. A cluttered terrarium does not look very nice, and you will have difficulty in maintaining it as well as difficulty in observing or even finding the animals!

Again, probably most experienced terrarium keepers prefer a spartan terrarium that is easy to clean and uncluttered. Plants cannot be sanitized to prevent entry of parasites and disease-causing organisms, and the soil in which they grow is literally alive with small plants and animals. Few plants really do well in terraria and most look awful in just a few days. Snakes really can become impaled on thorns of succulents (especially before shedding, when they may be virtually blind). Also, if your goal is to have a snake to look at every once in a while, if you give it too many hiding places — plants and their pots — you may never see it again without having to tear up the entire terrarium. A simple cage with paper on the bottom, a basking rock, a small hide box, a water bowl, and a climbing branch is your best bet, especially when starting out.

Yellow rat snake, *Elaphe obsoleta quadrivittata.* Before purchasing your pet snake, be sure you can meet its particular housing needs.

Nutrition

Albino California kingsnake feeding on a "pinkie" or newborn mouse.

All snakes are carnivorous; as they possess no grinding teeth, they must swallow their prey whole. In captivity, most species must be given whole prey, but there are some exceptions — fish-eating snakes, for example, will take strips of raw fish. Providing that acceptable prey items are readily available, consumption of whole prey by captive snakes has its advantages. With many other captive animals it is often necessary to prepare elaborate diets to ensure that they receive all of the important nutrients. All animals require the correct amounts of proteins, carbohydrates, fats, vitamins, trace elements (mineral salts), and water to allow their bodies to function efficiently. Providing the food items have themselves been reared on a balanced diet containing all of these essential ingredients, these will in themselves constitute a balanced diet for the snakes.

Variegated racer, *Coluber ravergieri.* The typical racer diet consists of small mammals, birds and their eggs, and small snakes.

BASIC FOODS

Of the different snake species, some have a fairly diversified diet and will consume a wide variety of prey items; in general, these are somewhat easier to cater to in captivity than the many others that have become completely or partially specialized and have limited food preferences. Snakes in this latter category should not be kept unless an adequate and regular supply of the prey or an acceptable substitute is available. Some species feed exclusively on frogs, others on salamanders or lizards; there are even those such as the king cobra, *Ophiophagus hannah,* that will feed almost exclusively on other snakes. Other unusual restricted feeders include egg-eating snakes (Dasypeltinae), crab-eaters (*Fordonia*), snail eaters (Dipsadinae), and termite-eaters (Leptotyphlopidae).

The vast majority of snake species kept in captivity are those with a wide diet preference and the ability to adapt readily to foods that can be easily obtained. Such items usually consist of fish, mice, rats, and chickens. All snakes catch and kill live prey in the wild, but the practice of giving live prey to captive snakes is often met with a great deal of opposition. Some snakes will take carrion in the wild, and the majority of captive snakes eventually can be persuaded to take dead prey, some more quickly than others. Newly captured specimens and recently hatched juveniles are often the most difficult to feed on dead food, but with a certain amount of patience and cajoling it is usually possible to get even the most stubborn of snakes to take dead prey. The following gives some ideas of how to obtain a range of food items.

Invertebrates: Many small species and the young of some larger ones will take various kinds of invertebrates. Slugs, snails, and earthworms are a favorite food of some types. Garter snakes (*Thamnophis*) are particularly fond of large earthworms. One method of ensuring a regular supply of earthworms is to turn over the soil in a corner of the garden and cover it with a 2-inch layer of dead leaves over which is placed a piece of burlap. The burlap is kept damp by daily watering. Worms will be attracted to the dampness and the dead leaves, and can be collected by rummaging about among them. Other kinds of invertebrates, including grasshoppers and crickets, may be collected by searching among thick undergrowth or by turning over rocks and rotting logs. Whenever feeding wild-caught food, be especially wary of contamination from insecticides (crickets and grasshoppers) and herbicides (earthworms). Snakes can be killed by very small poison residues in their food.

Fish: Many species of snake will feed on whole fish, and some will even take strips of fish muscle. Wherever possible, one should use freshwater fish species to feed snakes, as there is evidence to suggest that feeding marine fish leads to a deficiency of vitamin B in the diet. This is due to the fact that marine fish flesh contains an enzyme that prevents the

Garter snake, *Thamnophis sirtalis*. Members of this genus can be fed earthworms, fish, pinkies, strips of raw beef, and the occasional cricket.

utilization of the vitamin in the reptile's body. If there is no alternative to marine fish, strips of it should be held in boiling water for one minute and allowed to cool before feeding to the snake. This treatment destroys the enzyme that does the harm. The most satisfactory method of feeding fish to snakes is to give them live fish of a cheap and easy to breed variety. Your local pet shop is a good source of tropical fish such as goldfish and guppies, which are inexpensive to buy, but it may pay to have a couple of breeding tanks of these prolific livebearers in the home so that a steady supply is available. A goldfish farm is another ready source of useful fish prey for your snakes. Many breeders have to cull out a large number of misshapen fish each season and may be pleased to sell them off cheaply. The increasing number of trout farms that raise fish for

Yellow rat snake, *Elaphe obsoleta quadrivittata*. Keep in mind that captive snakes can easily become obese, since they do not get the exercise they would in the wild.

human consumption may also be willing to sell you numbers of fish of varying sizes from fry upward.

Amphibians: Many snakes specialize in eating frogs or salamanders. Such snakes should not be kept unless a steady supply of food items is available, remembering that many wild amphibian species are protected by law. If you have a pond in the back garden it may be a good idea to populate it with a stock of easy to breed amphibians so that a steady supply is available. Small leopard frogs (*Rana*) are available over much of the year from biological supply houses, as are newts, but purchasing them soon turns into a very expensive proposition.

Poultry: The domestic fowl is widely used in its various stages of growth as a convenient food for captive snakes. The advantages of these are that they are easy to obtain, come in various sizes, and are nutritious. Chick hatcheries frequently cull off batches of day-old chicks, and these can usually be obtained inexpensively. They can be kept alive and grown to various sizes, or they may be slaughtered and kept in the deep-freeze for future use. Some specialist suppliers deal in wholesale quantities of frozen chicks. Other kinds of poultry that may be used include ducks, geese, and quail; the latter are especially useful due to the small size of the chicks, making them suitable for quite small snakes. Be sure that frozen chicks — and any other frozen foods, for that matter — are *thoroughly* thawed before feeding.

Small Mammals: The staple diet of many thousands of pet snakes must be laboratory mice or rats that are bred in enormous numbers. Surplus stock usually can be obtained quite inexpensively. If you have a medical laboratory in your area that breeds small rodents, it is almost certain that a regular supply of surplus stock will be available. It is often cheaper and more convenient to obtain stock this way, as it is required, than to go to the trouble of maintaining a breeding colony of rats or mice in the home. Pet shops also often have mice or rats, as well as hamsters and gerbils, all of which are acceptable snake food. Wild mice and rats caught in traps are acceptable, although there is a risk of infecting the snakes with internal parasites. Large snakes may be fed upon rabbits, or

guinea pigs, also available from laboratories or from pet shops.

Most common snakes feed best on "pinkies" — young rodents that are still hairless and blind. Some pet shops that cater to herps sell frozen pinkies at reasonable prices. These are probably your preferred choice for corn snakes and milksnakes, many of which adapt well to frozen foods.

Feeding Techniques: There are a number of tips and a few precautions to make things easier when feeding captive snakes. These should be borne in mind to ensure that your specimens receive an adequate diet but, at the same time, do not allow any mishaps. Many captive speci-

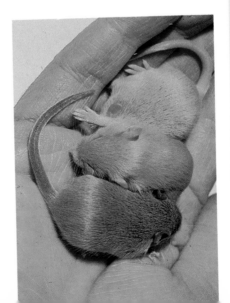

A trio of young mice. Some snake species will ignore dead food animals, while others will eat anything they can.

mens die prematurely due to a massive build-up of superfluous fat in the tissues caused by overfeeding. It is certainly quite exciting to own a snake that will eat almost as much as you care to give it, and it will grow rapidly, but remember that in the wild snakes have to hunt hard and long for their rations and are not programmed to a never-ending supply of plump laboratory reared animals! Therefore, use your common sense and only feed sparingly. Most snakes will thrive on a substantial meal every seven to ten days, although juvenile specimens should be given smaller meals more frequently during their main growing period. It takes a little practice and trial and error to get your snake's diet right but the reptile will benefit from the care and consideration.

If several snakes are kept together in a cage you must be extremely cautious at feeding time. If you feed your snakes on a regular basis, say once per week, the reptiles will learn to expect food at a certain time and will be ready and waiting as you open up the terrarium door. In the case of a "feeding frenzy" the snakes are likely to grab the first thing that comes into their cage, including your hand and each other. The danger is that two snakes could grab and attempt to swallow the same prey item, in which case there is a possibility of one reptile swallowing the other. When more than one snake is kept in a cage, it is best for them to be similar in size, the same species, and preferably a pair. Otherwise, the best policy is to keep each snake separately in a different cage unless mating is required. Where a number of snakes have to be kept together, one should attempt to feed each snake separately by removing all but one from the cage and feeding each in turn. It is important to keep a watch on the reptiles until all food items have been eaten, so that should anything unpleasant happen you are on the spot to sort it out. Any uneaten food should be removed from the cage within a few minutes. Never leave live rats or mice in with snakes; these are not unknown to have eaten into the flesh of a sick snake.

"It is certainly quite exciting to own a snake that will eat almost as much as you care to give it, and it will grow rapidly, but remember that in the wild snakes have to hunt hard and long for their rations and are not programmed to a never-ending supply of plump laboratory reared animals!"

44

Some species can be notoriously "difficult" feeders and take a great deal of cajoling to take food, especially when it is of an alien type different from what they are used to in the wild. The feeding habits of some species may play a part in their successful settlement in captivity. For example, the royal python, *Python regius,* will rarely take food from the floor of the cage, but if locked up in a small dark area with a dead mouse overnight, there is a good chance that it will eat. The author has been successful getting this species to feed by placing it in a small leather bag with a zipper and placing a dead mouse or small rat in with it. This indicates that in the wild this species normally hunts and overpowers prey in burrows and among tree roots.

Some snakes can be particularly obstinate and will refuse to feed willingly. The first thing to try in such a case is to take the food animal and move it about near to the reptile's snout, preferably with a stick. If this fails to produce a reaction, try tapping the snake on the nose with the food animal. If you are in luck, this will arouse the snake to angrily strike at the prey and, having had a taste, it may proceed to swallow it in the normal manner.

After all other methods of getting a snake to feed have failed, a *last resort* is force

A red milksnake, *Lampropeltis triangulum syspila*. This species often feeds on amphibians and lizards as well as earthworms and small mammals.

California kingsnake, *Lampropeltis getulus californiae*. The closer you can come to your pet's natural diet, the better off it will be.

feeding. There are two methods of doing this. In method one, pick the snake up behind the neck and, with the thumb and forefinger of the other hand, gently pinch the loose skin under the reptile's chin and pull the lower jaw open. The dead food animal can then be pushed (possibly by a second person) head first into the snake's gullet. Having pushed the food as far in as possible with the fingers, it may be gently forced further by using a wooden or plastic round-ended rod (the handle of a wooden spoon has proven useful) until the bulk of the prey is in the gullet. By massaging the snake's throat with the fingers, the prey can usually be coaxed further down into the system. In many cases the snake will begin to swallow the prey as soon as it is partially into the throat. A second and possibly more efficient method is to liquify the food item with a little water in a blender and then introduce it into the snake's system by means of a large syringe and a stomach tube. This method requires practice and skill.

Although some hobbyists see nothing wrong with occasionally force feeding a slow eater, there is certainly little to recommend continuous force feeding to maintain a snake that absolutely refuses to eat. Force feeding can be very stressful (to both snake and owner). If the non-feeding snake is locally caught it is best to simply release it before it becomes too weak to survive. Imported non-feeders sometimes will begin feeding if they are traded or sold into a new environment, but some individuals and some species simply would rather die than eat in captivity.

Snake Species

Oenpelli's python,
Python oenpelliensis.

In this chapter the types of snakes most suitable for the terrarium will be discussed. Species that are difficult to keep due to their specialized feeding or other habits have been omitted, as have venomous species other than a few mildly poisonous rear-fanged colubrid snakes.

BOAS AND PYTHONS (BOIDAE)

The family Boidae is split into several subfamilies, the most important being Boinae (typical boas) and Pythoninae (typical pythons). These are regarded as the giants of the snake world and contain species recorded in excess of 33 feet, although there are several species which do not grow beyond 24 inches. The Boinae are found mainly in the New World, with the main headquarters being in tropical South America; there are, however, a few

47

small species found in Madagascar, Africa, and Asia. The Pythoninae are confined to the tropical regions of the Old World, including Africa, Asia, and Australia. All are powerful constrictors, but the differences between the two main subfamilies include anatomical variations of the tooth-bearing bones and other skull structures. The pythons are also invariably egglayers (oviparous) while the boas are usually livebearers (ovoviviparous).

It is quite clear that the larger species of boas and pythons must have heavy-duty housing with thick glass. Special decorations are not essential; indeed, it would be a waste of time trying to grow plants in a cage containing such large snakes. In most cases a substrate of coarse gravel is adequate. A large water container, preferably a baby's bath tub or child's swimming pool, or even a drainable concrete pond, is a must, remembering that many boids like to spend long periods immersed in the water. As this water is also used for drinking, it is obvious that it must be frequently changed, refilling with water that has been heated to a lukewarm temperature, thus avoiding thermal shock. Most boids are adept climbers, and stout climbing branches must be provided. These are particularly important for such species as the green tree python, *Chondropython viridis,* which spends all of its time in the branches. The air temperature in the boid terrarium should be maintained around 79-84°F (26-29°C) during the day, allowing it to sink to room temperature, about 68°F (20°C), at night.

The boids are primarily

Green tree python, *Chondropython viridis*. This species has become endangered in recent years.

crepuscular (active at dusk and dawn) or nocturnal, therefore food should preferably be introduced in the evening. Always keep snakes under supervision at feeding time and be sure that two snakes do not start feeding on the same prey. Should this happen, they may be persuaded to release it by blowing tobacco smoke into their faces.

The most well known of all the giant snakes, although by far not the largest, is the boa constrictor, *Boa constrictor,* which is . Ind in tropical America from north-central Mexico south as far as Paraguay and northern Argentina. The snakes are beautifully marked in cream and russet brown.

Newly born juveniles about 16 inches in length are popular and may be reared on mice. They grow rapidly and if handled regularly will tame nicely. At the end of the first year they may reach about 4 feet in length. The maximum size of an adult boa constrictor is about 13 feet.

The heaviest of all the giant snakes, if not the longest, is the common or green anaconda, which is found in the basins of the Amazon and the Orinoco in tropical South America. Many tall stories exist about the length of an adult anaconda, but specimens 22-26 feet long are recorded with certainty and there is a well documented case of a specimen reaching 30.5 feet. More doubtful records to over 37 feet are known. The ground color of the anaconda is olive brown or green. There are two rows of dark spots extending along the flanks and a dark stripe passes through the eye extending toward the neck. Anacondas are water-loving snakes never found far from ponds or rivers. In the

Boa constrictor, *Boa constrictor.* In the past this species was known as *Constrictor constrictor.*

49

Fischer's or Haitian boa, *Epicrates striatus*.

all the colors of the rainbow. Smaller than many boids, this species reaches a maximum length of about 6.5 feet. It may be fed on mice and chicks. A closely related but somewhat larger species is the Haitian or Fischer's boa, *Epicrates striatus*. This species is attractively marked in reddish brown on a beige background. Several subspecies are found on various Caribbean islands. Maximum length is about 6 to 7 feet.

One of the most attractive of all boas is the emerald tree boa, *Corallus caninus,* from the tropical rain forests of South America. This species is totally arboreal and even has some difficulty in locomotion when it finds itself on the ground. The newly born young are brick red in color with yellow markings along the dorsal ridge; as they grow and change their skins they gradually take on the leaf-green adult color with small white or yellow markings. This may take three years. Maximum length is about 10 feet. In the wild this species feeds mainly on bats and birds. In captivity they tend

terrarium they will spend hours soaking in the water container. It is essential that the water be heated, otherwise the snakes will chill and refuse all food. Food consists of chickens, ducks, and rabbits. Juvenile specimens may be reared on fish, mice, and rats. Many specimens are vicious and virtually untamable. Because of their size, a bite from even a juvenile specimen can be serious, especially if secondary infections set in. Anacondas are not for beginners.

A popular species found from Central America through much of South America is the rainbow boa, *Epicrates cenchris.* Although the basic color is brown marked with darker rings, when viewed in a certain light a beautiful sheen shows to prefer chicks but can be trained to take mice or small rats.

The dwarfs among the boas include the various Afro-Asian sand boas, *Eryx*. These rarely grow to more than 3 feet in total length and spend much of their time buried under loose earth, sand, or leaf litter. In the terrarium they should be provided with a mixture of coarse sand, peat, and leaf litter to a depth of 8 inches. They may be fed upon mice. The most well known species are the European spotted sand boa, *Eryx jaculus,* from southeastern Europe and Asia Minor, and the brown sand boa, *Eryx johni,* found from Asia Minor to India.

Two species of boas are found in North America. The rosy boa, *Lichanura trivirgata,* inhabits desert and semidesert areas from Baja California to the southwestern U.S.A. The pale gray-blue to tan ground color of the body is broken with three reddish brown, often zig-zag, stripes. This is a popular terrarium subject that rarely exceeds 3 feet in length. It may be fed on mice. The rubber boa,

Charina bottae, bears a resemblance to the Asian sand boas (to which it is closely related), although its habitat is much different. It is found from the damp evergreen forests of the northwestern United States to the cool interior plains of Utah. When threatened, this species rolls its body into a ball, leaving the stubby head-like tail on the outside.

The subfamily Pythoninae contains some seven genera, the most well known of which is the genus *Python,* which extends from tropical Africa through to Southeast Asia to Australia. The reticulated python, *Python*

Juvenile sand boa, *Eryx johni*. The tail of this species is marked like its head in order to confuse predators.

reticulatus, from the rain forests of Southeast Asia, is the world's longest snake; the largest confirmed specimen, taken in the Philippine Islands, measured in excess of 33 feet. Such specimens can be dangerous to humans, and there are authenticated cases of people (usually children) being overpowered and eaten. Juveniles of this species are frequently available on the market. These are usually about 3 feet in length and may be fed on mice and small rats. As they grow, they will graduate to chickens and rabbits. Large specimens should be handled with care and kept only by experienced herpetologists.

Perhaps the most popular and well known member of the python subfamily is the Asiatic rock python, *Python molurus.* There are two subspecies, the tiger or Indian python, *P. m. molurus,* and the Burmese python, *P. m. bivittatus,* the former from the Indian subcontinent, the latter from Burma and Malaysia and also Southeast Asia. Burmese pythons are the most prolific of captive breeders. Females will steadfastly brood their clutch of eggs even in a terrarium on public display. Newly hatched specimens are about 2 feet in length and may be fed on mice. They quickly become excellent pets even at their adult size of 13-16 feet. Even larger specimens are sometimes seen.

Closely related to the preceding species is the African rock python, *Python sebae,* which is found over most parts of Africa south of

Indian rock python, *Python molurus molurus*. This species has been called the most "trustworthy" member of its genus.

the Sahara Desert.
Specimens in excess of 26
feet in length have been
recorded. This species is
somewhat more irritable than
the Asiatic rock python and
should be handled with care.
Both species will feed on
mice, chicks, rats, chickens,
and rabbits, depending on
the sizes.

Another African species,
the royal or ball python,
Python regius, found in the
rain forests, barely reaches 6
feet in length. It is
attractively marked in cream,
black, and chocolate brown.
Although this species
sometimes takes badly to
capture, once settled into
captivity it makes an
excellent and docile pet. It
feeds mainly on small
rodents.

Of the several species of
Australian pythons, the
carpet python, *Python
(Morelia) spilotes,* and its
color variety the diamond
python are the best known.
Reaching a length of about
13-16 feet but somewhat
slim, they may be fed on rats
and chickens.

Finally, a section on
pythons would be incomplete
without mention of the
Papuan green tree python,

Chondrophython viridis,
from New Guinea and parts
of northern Australia. This
species bears a remarkable
resemblance to the emerald
tree boa, *Corallus caninus,*
and has almost identical
habits and colors, even down
to the young being brick red
in color. As with other
pythons, however, it lays
eggs, unlike the boa, which
bears live young.

TYPICAL SNAKES (COLUBRIDAE)

More than two-thirds of
living snakes belong to the
family Colubridae, of which

African rock python,
*Python sebae
natalensis.* This
species is one of the
more slender
members of its
genus.

53

Viperine snake, *Natrix maura*. Members of the genus *Natrix* are excellent swimmers.

authorities today feel this subfamily should not be recognized. There are some notable exceptions to the general harmlessness of colubrids, including the boomslang, *Dispholidus typus,* and the twig snake, *Thelotornus kirtlandii,* both from Africa, which have caused human deaths and are definitely not recommended for the home terrarium. Many other instances of isolated venomous effects from bites of normally non-venomous species (such as hognosed snakes and water snakes) are recorded in the literature. With so many species in the family Colubridae, it is not surprising that there is a considerable range of specialization. Some of them are difficult to keep in captivity due to their specialized feeding habits, whereas others are relatively easy.

In Europe, one of the most well known species is the Eurasian grass snake, *Natrix natrix* (called the Eurasian water snake by Americans), which is olive brown in color marked with black dots and with a distinctive yellow collar. Being semiaquatic,

there are some 2300 species, most of which can be described as "typical" and harmless. The group forms the dominant element of the snake faunas of all continents with the exception of Australia, where the venomous elapids are in the majority. Many subfamilies are recognized by various authorities, the most important being the Colubrinae, containing the vast majority of harmless (non-venomous) snakes. The rear-fanged snakes, most of which are relatively harmless to humans as their mouths are too small to bite, or the venom is not very powerful, were once put in a subfamily Boiginae, but most this species, which grows to about 5 feet in length, requires a medium-sized aqua-terrarium. It may be fed on fish and frogs and should be kept at a summer daytime temperature of 77°F, reduced at night. As with many other snakes from temperate areas, it will benefit from a winter "hibernation" period at a reduced temperature. Closely related to the grass snake are the tesselated water snake, *Natrix tesselata,* and the viperine snake (so named after its squat, viper-like body), *Natrix maura.* Both these species, from central and southern Europe, require similar care, though slightly higher summer temperatures.

In North America several species of water snake in the genus *Nerodia* also require similar care. The best known is the common water snake, *Nerodia sipedon,* found in the eastern half of the U.S.A. from Canada to the Gulf. The ground color is olive-green to brown, marked with dark bands and zig-zags. It grows to about 4 feet in length. The largest North American water snake is the green water snake, *Nerodia cyclopion,* which

reaches some 6 feet in length.

Some of the most suitable colubrid snakes for the terrarium belong to the genus *Elaphe,* which has several well known species from Europe and North America. One of the most popular and beautiful is the corn snake, *Elaphe guttata,* which is found over much of the eastern and central United States. It is attractively marked in red and black and grows to about 6 feet. Easy to feed on mice, the corn snake makes a docile and ideal terrarium subject. Another group of North American snakes that are widely kept are the rat snakes, *Elaphe obsoleta,* of which there are several subspecies, distributed over the entire eastern United

Rat snake, *Elaphe obsoleta obsoleta*. This species is commonly found in farm areas.

The yellow rat snake,
*Elaphe obsoleta
quadrivittata*, often
occurs in damp,
humid climates.

States. Particularly popular is the yellow rat snake, *E. o. quadrivittata.* Reaching a length of 6-8 feet, they may be fed on mice, small rats and chicks.

Several *Elaphe* species occur in Europe and Asia. A popular member of the genus *Elaphe* in Europe is the Aesculapean snake, *Elaphe longissima,* which reaches some 6.5 feet in length. It is a good terrarium subject, soon settling into captivity and feeding on mice and small rats. It requires a roomy terrarium with rocks and climbing branches. The four-lined snake, *Elaphe quatuorlineata,* is a close relative requiring similar care. This species reaches a length of 8 feet and may be as much as 4 inches in diameter at its thickest point. Similar in appearance to the corn snake but more slimly built is the leopard snake, *Elaphe situla.* This species is a little more difficult to maintain in captivity but will usually settle down to feed on mice. Another closely related species is the ladder snake, *Elaphe scalaris,* with its ladder-like markings on a gray background.

Very popular are the North American snakes known as the kingsnakes and milksnakes, *Lampropeltis.* Although they eat other snakes, including rattlesnakes, usually their main diet is small rodents and lizards. They are powerful constrictors and can overpower prey larger than themselves. The common kingsnake, *Lampropeltis getulus,* includes several subspecies, the most popular being the California king, *L. g. californiae;* the speckled king, *L. g. holbrooki,* and the Florida king, *L. g. floridana.* All require a roomy terrarium with rocks and climbing branches. They will feed on mice, rats, chicks, or indeed, almost anything that moves. They grow to about 6-7 feet in length.

While the common kingsnake is marked in various combinations of black, brown, and yellow or white, the closely related milksnakes or scarlet kingsnakes, *Lampropeltis triangulum,* are a riot of color with bands of yellow, black, and red. They are called milksnakes because of the still widely held belief that the snakes drink milk from the udders of cows. Milksnakes are interesting, docile, and colorful pets. Keep most subspecies at 82°F maximum, 68°F minimum. Many restrictions on possession and sale of *Lampropeltis* species are now applied at both local and national levels because they have been overcollected in the past. Captive-bred specimens of many subspecies are now becoming widely available.

Racers and whipsnakes, genus *Coluber,* are also encountered both in North America and Eurasia. In most of the United States the common racer, *Coluber constrictor,* is well known. It is a long, slender snake reaching 6 feet in length and, as its common name implies, it is a fast mover. A familiar European species is the green whip snake, *Coluber viridiflavus,* which is colored green and yellow.

Mexican milksnake, *Lampropeltis trangulum annulata.*

Speckled racer,
Drymobius
margaritiferus.

Coluber constrictor is considered to be a very nervous species that does not adapt well to captivity and is virtually never offered on the pet market.

One of the most popular snakes, which unfortunately may have led in part to its scarcity in the wild, is the eastern indigo snake, *Drymarchon corais couperi*. Found in the southeastern United States, it was formerly collected extensively for the pet trade. Now it is fortunately protected in the wild state, but there is a fair amount of captive-bred stock available from time to time. The eastern indigo snake grows to almost 10 feet in length and is North America's longest snake. It has a beautiful sheen to its blue-black skin and is red under the chin. Indigo snakes should preferably be kept on their own outside the breeding season as they will eat other snakes and have been known to eat each other. The species as a whole ranges from southern Texas to Argentina with *D. c. couperi* quite isolated from the rest of the species. Mexican subspecies of the indigo snake are often available but are not as attractive as the *couperi* type.

Ideal for beginners are the various North American garter snakes in the genus *Thamnophis*. So small and easy to feed, they only require a modest terrarium with basking areas. Being semiaquatic, they can be kept in a converted aquarium with equal amounts of land and water. One nice thing about garter snakes is that they will feed on a diet of earthworms and strips of dead fish, although in the latter case vitamin and mineral supplements must be provided.

An African colubrid that is popular and frequently available is the mole snake, *Pseudaspis cana*. This species can be somewhat irritable when first captured and will bite readily, but it will soon settle into captivity. This chestnut brown snake grows to about 5 feet in length. It is found in the drier areas of the

southern half of Africa. Another African snake with interesting feeding habits is the egg-eater, *Dasypeltis scabra,* which feeds exclusively on bird eggs. In captivity it may be fed on pigeon or quail eggs.

Several rear-fanged and mildly venomous snakes make interesting and colorful terrarium inmates, although they must be handled carefully. In particular, the various tree snakes of

Common garter snake, *Thamnophis sirtalis*. Garter snakes are very hardy and are relatively easy to breed.

Dog-toothed mangrove snake, *Boiga cynodon*. This species ranges from Burma to the Indo-Australian archipelago.

Above and left:
The long-nosed tree snake, *Ahaetulla prasina*, is active during daylight hours. It mainly feeds on lizards.

Mangrove snake, *Boiga drapiezii.* This species is a nocturnal tree-dweller.

The flying snake, *Chrysopelia ornata,* is a sun-worshipper that hunts for lizards in the treetops.

Southeast Asia are very popular. Requiring a temperature of 77-86°F and a high humidity, these snakes require climbing branches. One of the largest is the vivid yellow and black mangrove snake, *Boiga dendrophila,* which can reach 6.5 feet in length. It may be fed on chicks or mice, but seems to prefer the former. More difficult to feed is the long-nosed tree snake, *Ahaetulla nasuta,* which feeds mainly on small lizards and frogs in the wild. In captivity it can be trained to take small live fish such as guppies from a shallow water container. One of the most exciting of snakes is the so-called flying snake, *Chrysopelia ornata,* which moves speedily through the trees, launching itself from branches and gliding down to a lower level by using air resistance on its concave belly surface. These colorful green and yellow snakes can be fed on mice. Although only mildly venomous, all rear-fanged snakes should be handled with the utmost caution as there are always those people who are somewhat more allergic to venoms than are others.

Above: Green mangrove snake, *Boiga cyanea*. This species' diet includes venomous snakes.

Left: Green tree python, *Chondropython viridis*.

63

Index